Presented by:

_____

To:

_____

Date:

_____

Occasion:

_____

Wings for
the Soul

"99 Words to Live By"

A series of fine gift books that presents inspirational words by renowned authors and captivating thinkers. Thought-provoking proverbs from many peoples and traditions complete each volume's collection.

"99 Words to Live By" explores topics that have moved and will continue to move people's hearts. Perfect for daily reflection as well as moments of relaxation.

Wings for the Soul

99 Sayings on Happiness

edited by
Anne Bryan Smollin

New City Press
Hyde Park, New York

Published in the United States by New City Press
202 Cardinal Rd., Hyde Park, NY 12538
©2008 Anne Bryan Smollin

Cover design by Leandro de Leon

Library of Congress Cataloging-in-Publication Data:

Wings for the soul : 99 sayings on happiness / edited by Anne
Bryan Smollin.
       p. cm. -- (99 words to live by)
    ISBN 978-1-56548-283-8 (hardcover : alk. paper) --
ISBN 978-1-56548-284-5 (pbk. : alk. paper) 1. Happiness--
Quotations, maxims, etc. I. Smollin, Anne Bryan.

BJ1481.W74 2008
170'.44--dc22   2007028664

Printed in United States of America

Everyone wants to be happy, and everyone can be. We often look for happiness in the externals around us — if my children were all settled then I'd be happy; if we could win the lottery … ; if I had a better job … ; if someone would love me more — thinking that these will bring us happiness.

When I visit Peru I meet people with little water and few material possessions, and who struggle to provide food for their families, yet they have immense joy and happiness. We find the key to happiness not outside ourselves in what we have or don't have, but within. If we choose to be happy, we keep our attitudes positive and think outside ourselves. We give our time away; we offer to be present to another in need; we like the person we see in the mirror; we respect and accept what each moment holds for us. When we catch the breath and energy of each moment, we feel content and joy graces our lives.

Happiness doesn't really lie in 99 sayings, but perhaps these can aid us on our journey.

For each of the favorite quotes I have chosen from many sources, I have given credit.

Any saying for which no source is listed comes from my own writing on happiness and joy. My hope and prayer is that you begin to write your own prescriptions for happiness.

Anne Bryan Smollin

Happiness is something that comes into our lives through doors we don't even remember leaving open.

Rose Wilder Lane
American Writer and Journalist

Happiness is
looking for something
to be surprised at everyday.

Happiness is
a perfume you cannot
pour on others without
getting a few drops
on yourself.

Ralph Waldo Emerson

Happiness is
often found
in the unexpected.

Fragrance always
clings to the hand
that gives you roses.

Chinese Proverb

Happiness is
finding beauty
in a place or person
we never expected
to find beauty at all.

Happiness
is not in the mere
possession of money;
it lies in the joy
of achievement,
in the thrill
of creative effort.

Franklin D. Roosevelt

Happiness is
found in what you have
— not in what you want.

True happiness
is not attained through
self-gratification,
but through fidelity
to a worthy purpose.

Helen Keller

Happiness is yours
when you know your life
has meaning and purpose.

Part of the happiness
of life consists
not in fighting battles
but in avoiding them.

Vincent Peale

Happiness is
when we can say
"I'm sorry" and let
the healing begin.

Happiness is
the supreme good:
It is so important
that all else
is merely a means
to its attainment.

Aristotle

Happiness doesn't depend on what is happening but in how we see what is happening.

Happy the one who
finds wisdom, the man
who gains understanding!
For her profit is better than
profit in silver, and better than
gold is her revenue;
She is more precious than
corals, and none
of your choice possessions
can compare with her.

Proverbs 3:13-15

Happiness means
we know we may
not be able to control
what happens but
we can decide how
we want to behave
and act and think.

Happiness makes up
in height for what
it lacks in length.

Robert Frost

Just for today
I will be happy
knowing that
I am created
for happiness

John XXIII

The supreme
happiness in life
is the conviction
that we are loved.

Victor Hugo

Happiness is
having someone
tell you that you made
a difference in their life.

Most folks are
about as happy
as they make up
their minds to be.

Abraham Lincoln

Happiness is

knowing someone
is thinking about you,

knowing someone
misses you,

knowing someone
wants to be with you,

knowing someone
loves you.

To get up each morning
with the resolve
to be happy … is to set
our own conditions
to the events of each day.
To do this is to
condition circumstances
instead of being
conditioned by them.

Ralph Waldo Emerson

Pursuing happiness
is a matter of choice …
a positive attitude
we choose to find
in each moment.

Good memories
are our second chance
at happiness.

Queen Elizabeth II

Happiness is getting an invitation to a picnic and meeting up with people who give us memories to hold in our minds for the whole year. The very thought of them bring a smile to our faces. Maybe these memories are given to us in the warmth of the summer so we can hold them to our hearts in the cold of the winter.

We are never happy
for a thousand days,
a flower never blooms
for a hundred.

Chinese Proverb

Most of us
miss happiness
because we are so busy
living our own agendas
we don't see what
is in front of us.

When one door
of happiness closes,
another opens;
but often we look so long
at the closed door
that we do not see
the one which
has opened for us.

Helen Keller

Happiness is
telling someone
something without
using words.

Happy those who do not follow the counsel of the wicked, nor go the way of sinners, nor sit in company with scoffers.

Rather, the law of the Lord is their joy; God's law they study day and night.

They are like a tree planted near streams of water, that yields its fruit in season; Its leaves never wither; whatever they do prospers.

Psalm 1:1-2

Happiness means
we can be vulnerable
and take a risk.

If I had but two
loaves of bread,
I would sell one
and buy hyacinths,
for they would
feed my soul.

Q'uran

We often block
happiness
not by what we eat
but what we allow
to eat us.

If you want
to be happy, be.

Leo Tolstoy

Happiness is
remembering
I am only human …
I don't have to be perfect.

In the judgment,
we will be
held accountable
for every blessing
we refused to enjoy.

Jewish Proverb

We experience
happiness when we learn
to laugh at ourselves.

He deserves paradise
who makes
his companions laugh.

Q'uran

One of the greatest gifts we can give to another is the gift of laughter. Laughter is an activity of the heart. It makes a noise so others can hear our feelings. Laughter tickles our very souls. It helps us to live happier and helps those around us enjoy us even more.

Lord give me
a sense of humor
so that I may take some
happiness from this life
and share it with others.

St. Thomas More

Happiness
never diminishes
by being shared.

Time spent laughing is time spent with the gods.

Japanese Proverb

Take time to laugh.
It is the music of the soul.

Irish Prayer

Joy, gratitude and love
cultivate happiness.

A kindly glance
gives joy to the heart,
good news lends strength
to the bones

Proverbs 15:30

Peace starts with a smile.

Mother Teresa of Calcutta

God fills our mouth
with laughter.

Job 8:21

A smile creates
happiness in a home,
positive feelings
in the work place,
and connectedness
in the community.

God, deliver me from sullen saints.

Teresa of Avila

The fullness of joy
is to behold God
in everything.

Julian of Norwich

Joy does not simply
happen to us.
We have to choose joy
and keep choosing it
every day.

Henri Nouwen

Happiness is appreciating little things in our life like flowers, sunrises, changing leaves, and the beauty of the first snowfall. It is found in the smile of a baby and the twinkling eyes of an aged person.

Happy the person
whose longing for God
is like the passion
of a lover for her beloved.

St. John Climacus

Happiness is
remembering that God
calls us by name.

The joy of the Lord
is your strength.

Nehemiah 8:10

We need to stop, to let go of all the surface stuff, and go into the desert of our heart. And listen. Then knowing our emptiness and deepest longings, we must seek the prophetic wisdom that can point the way. If we do not take time to listen to our deepest longings, if we constantly drown them out with our activities and distractions, we can never hope to find true happiness.

M. Basil Pennington

Happiness is
not in externals
but inside of us.

Kowing that we are children of God: this certantity is the unfailing spring of our joy…. It makes us sad to realize that God is so good to us while we are so unworthy. Still, even such sadness turns sweet.

John XXIII

Sometimes your joy
is the source of your smile,
but sometimes your smile
can be the source of your joy.

Thich Nhat Hanh

The fruit of humilty and compassion is joy.

Henri Nouwen

A merry heart is
the life of the flesh.

Proverbs 14:30

Rejoice in the Lord always. I shall say it again: rejoice! Your kindness should be known to all. The Lord is near. Have no anxiety at all, but in everything, by prayer and petition, with thanksgiving, make your requests known to God.

Then the peace of God that surpasses all understanding will guard your hearts and minds in Christ Jesus.

Philippians 4:4-7

Happiness is
living the present
moment fully.
It means letting
go of the past and
not worrying
about the future.

When one is gloomy
everything seems
to go wrong;
when one is cheerful,
everything seems right.

Proverbs 15:15

Spend time with a child;
hold the hand of
an older person;
listen to someone in need
— you then know
what happiness is.

Kind words
can be short
and easy to speak,
but their echoes
are truly endless.

Mother Teresa of Calcutta

Our life is what
our thoughts make it.

Marcus Aurelius

Happiness is
remembering our blessings
outnumber our difficulties.

Resolve to keep happy
and your joy shall form
an invincible host
against difficulties.

Helen Keller

Pain has a paradoxical purpose: it is the channel to happiness, if we are speaking of true happiness and lasting happiness, and not a fleeting, or provisional one. We are speaking of that one happiness alone that can satisfy the human heart, the very happiness God enjoys and which human beings, for the transcendent destiny that is theirs, can already share in this life.

Chiara Lubich

Affirming and praising another is extending joy and happiness to that person.

The best way to show our gratitude to God and to people is to accept everything with joy. A joyful heart is the inevitable result of a heart burning with love. Never let anything so fill you with sorrow as to make you forget the joy of Christ Risen.

Mother Teresa of Calcutta

"A happy man or woman
is a radiant focus
of good will,
and their entrance
into a room is as though
another had been lighted."

Robert Louis Stevenson

The surest way
to happiness is to feel
connected to others.

A happy family
is but an earlier heaven.

Chinese Proverb

Happiness is knowing our guardian angel is always next to us and protecting us. Sometimes the angel comes as an aged person; sometimes the angel is in a message; and sometimes we just feel taken care of.

I have never been hurt
by anything I didn't say.

Calvin Collidge

Finally, brothers, whatever is true, whatever is honorable, whatever is just, whatever is pure, whatever is lovely, whatever is gracious, if there is any excellence and if there is anything worthy of praise, think about these things.

Keep on doing what you have learned and received and heard and seen in me.

Then the God of peace will be with you.

Philippians 4:8-9

A simple "thank-you"
or "please" can turn
a person's day around.

He who lives
in harmony with himself
lives in harmony
with the universe.

Marcus Aurelius

A kind heart is
a fountain of gladness,
making everything
in its vicinity
freshen into smiles.

Washington Irving

Light does not mean that
there is not more night.
But it does mean
that the night is bright
and can be overcome.

Heinrich Fries

I think I began learning
long ago that those
who are happiest
are those who do
the most for others.

Booker T. Washington

When you
give something away —
you always get it back.
Bring some joy
and happiness
into another's life
and watch what
you get back.

After having
given us Jesus,
God bestows on us
the greatest gift —
the Holy Spirit.
In turn, we are called
to give ourselves freely,
with generosity and joy,
to God and to neighbor.

Mother Teresa of Calcutta

Doing something
for someone who
can not repay you
is what happiness
is all about.

Let us be
grateful to people
who make us happy;
they are the charming
gardeners who make
our souls blossom.

Marcel Proust

Service which
is rendered without joy
helps neither the servant
nor the served.
But all other pleasures
and possessions pale into
nothingness before service
which is rendered
in a spirit of joy.

Mohandas K. Gandhi

No act of kindness,
no matter how small,
is ever wasted.

Aesop

It's not what we have
that makes us happy
but what we give.

Make happy
those who are near
and those who are far
will come.

Chinese Proverb

People act
more kindly and lovingly
when they are happy.
Unhappy people
are too preoccupied
with themselves.

Maybe this is why God commanded us to love: so that he can give us the joy of feeling we are children, not of limited and powerless human beings, but children of God, of the King of kings.

Chiara Lubich

If you want
others to be happy,
practice compassion.
If you want to be happy,
practice compassion.

Dalai Lama

Everlasting joy consists of: recognizing and loving transparent truth, and the Word of God, and the Wisdom through which all things were made, and his extraordinary loving kindness.

Augustine of Hippo

Wouldn't we live
in a happier world
if we spent more time
thanking one another and
expressing gratitude
rather than being negative,
sarcastic, and rude
to each other?

The world is made up of unhappy people because humankind has not recognized the source of its happiness. The stars shine in the sky and the earth stays in existence because they are in motion: movement is the life of the universe. People are truly happy only if they turn on the motor of their lives, love, and keep it running.

Chiara Lubich

Let no one ever
come to you
without leaving you
better and happier.

Mother Teresa of Calcutta

Also available in the same series:

On Our Pilgrimage to Eternity
99 Sayings by John Paul II
hardcover: 1-56548-198-4
softcover: 1-56548-230-1

Words of Hope and Healing
99 Sayings by Henri Nouwen
hardcover: 1-56548-227-1

Like a Drop in the Ocean
99 Sayings by Mother Teresa
hardcover: 1-56548-238-7
softcover: 1-56548-242-5

The Path of Merciful Love
99 Sayings by Thérèse of Lisieux
hardcover: 1-56548-245-X
softcover: 1-56548-246-8

Overlook Much Correct a Little
99 Sayings by John XXIII
hardcover: 13: 978-1-56548-261-6
softcover: 13: 978-1-56548-255-5

Coming Together in Joy
99 Sayings by Benedict XVI
hardcover: 978-1-56548-273-9
softcover: 978-1-56548-274-6

* * *

The Golden Thread of Life
99 Sayings on Love
hardcover: 1-56548-182-8

Blessed Are the Peacemakers
99 Sayings on Peace
hardcover: 1-56548-183-6

Sunshine On Our Way
99 Sayings on Friendship
hardcover: 1-56548-195-X

We Have Seen a Great Light
99 Sayings on Christmas
hardcover: 978-1-56548-270-8
softcover: 978-1-56548-271-5 (September 2008)

Organizations and Corporations

This title is available at special quantity discounts for bulk purchases for sales promotions, premiums, or fundraising. For information call or write:

New City Press, Marketing Dept.
202 Cardinal Rd.
Hyde Park, NY 12538.
Tel: 1-800-462-5980;
1-845-229-0335
Fax: 1-845-229-0351
info@newcitypress.com